**Books should be returned on or before the
last date stamped below.**

**ABERDEENSHIRE LIBRARY
AND INFORMATION SERVICE
MELDRUM MEG WAY, OLDMELDRUM**

Buddhist Temples

Andrea Willson

Heinemann
LIBRARY

First published in Great Britain by Heinemann Library
Halley Court, Jordan Hill, Oxford OX2 8EJ
a division of Reed Educational and Professional Publishing Ltd.
Heinemann is a registered trademark of Reed Educational & Professional Publishing Limited.

OXFORD MELBOURNE AUCKLAND
JOHANNESBURG IBADAN BLANTYRE GABORONE
PORTSMOUTH NH (USA) CHICAGO

Designed by Tinstar Design (www.tinstar.co.uk)
Illustrations by Martin Griffin and Nicholas Beresford-Davies
Printed by South China Printing in Hong Kong / China

02 01 00 99 98
10 9 8 7 6 5 4 3 2 1

J294.34
1171146

British Library Cataloguing in Publication Data

Willson, Andrea
    Buddhist Temples. - (Places of worship)
    1. Temples, Buddhist - Juvenile literature
    I. Title
    294.5'35

ISBN 0 431 05185 2

Acknowledgements

The Publishers would like to thank the following for permission to reproduce photographs and artwork:
Andes Press Agency/C & D Hill, p.4; Andes Press Agency/Carlos Reyes-Manzo, pp.6 (left), 10, 11, 19, 20, 21;
Bath, Robin, pp.7, 8, 9, 12, 14, 16, 18; Circa Photo Library/William Holtby, p.15; Emmett, Phil & Val, p.13
(left); Samye Ling Tibetan Centre/Leon Maurice, p.6; Tibet Images/Brian Beresford, p.17; Weber, Andy, pp.12
(top), 13 (right); Weber, Liza, p.11 (bottom).

Cover photograph of the Buddhist temple in Wimbledon, reproduced with permission of Robert Harding Picture
Library/G.R. Richardson.

Our thanks to Philip Emmett for his comments in the preparation of this book, and to Louise Spilsbury for all
her hard work.

The author would like to dedicate this book to Liza and her friends at Leven Valley School.

Contents

Words printed in **bold letters like these**
are explained in the Glossary.

What is a Buddhist temple?

A temple is a building where **Buddhists** come to pray and **meditate**. Buddhists are people who follow the teachings of Siddhartha Gautama, a man they call the **Buddha**.

Most Buddhists live in Asian countries like Thailand and Japan. Their temples are built to look special, often using gold and decorative designs.

This temple is in Thailand.

Buddhists in Britain

The Buddha lived in India about 2500 years ago. His teachings spread to other countries like China, Japan, Sri Lanka, Burma and Tibet. Now **Buddhism** is popular all over the world.

These maps show you India, where Buddhism began. They also show how the religion spread.

Temples in Britain

There are many different kinds of **Buddhist** temples in Britain. This is because **Buddhism** came to Britain from many different countries. For instance, if a Buddhist group comes from Vietnam, then their temple will be built like the ones in that country.

Two different Buddhist temples in Britain.

Dharma centres

Some temples are just special rooms inside new or old buildings. The building may also have other useful rooms like an office and a library.

These places are called **Dharma** Centres. Buddhists meet at these centres and study the Dharma together. Dharma is the name given to the teachings of the **Buddha**.

There are over 350 Buddhist groups and Dharma Centres in Britain today. Only the bigger, older organizations have separate temples.

Buddhists meeting at a Dharma centre.

Let's look inside

Before you go into a temple, you take your shoes off and leave them outside the door. This keeps the room clean and shows your respect.

Some people might be in the temple praying or **meditating** so you need to be quiet. There are usually cushions on the floor for people to sit on. But there are often a few chairs for those who prefer them.

Inside a temple.

What can you see?

The most important part of the temple is the **shrine**. The shrine is in the front, at the centre of the temple. It holds **images** of the **Three Jewels**. This is the name given to the three most respected things in **Buddhism**. These are the **Buddha**, the **Dharma** and the **Sangha**.

Sangha usually means **Buddhist** teachers, **monks** and **nuns**, but can mean all a person's Buddhist friends.

Some shrines are simple, others hold many special objects. Behind some are beautiful paintings of **buddhas**.

When Buddhists come into a temple, they bow or **prostrate** in front of the shrine as a sign of respect.

The Buddha

The most important object you see in a temple is the statue of the **Buddha**. The Buddha was a good, kind and wise prince who wanted to discover the meaning of life. He left home and **meditated** for a long time until he finally became **enlightened**. This means that he came to a state of perfect kindness and understanding. Buddha means 'enlightened one' in English.

Many temples show events in the life of the Buddha as a reminder of important **Buddhist** teachings.

Offerings to Buddha

Offerings are objects like flowers, **incense** or food placed on the **shrine**. Buddhists believe that making offerings encourages them to be kind and generous, like the Buddha. Making offerings also shows their respect for the Buddha.

Long ago people welcomed special guests by offering them pleasant things. These were water for washing and drinking, flowers, perfume, light, incense and food. Buddhists now place seven small bowls of fresh water in front of **images** of Buddha as **symbols** of these gifts.

Offerings on a shrine to Buddha.

Perfume

Dolly

Lipstick

Mermaid

Apples in a bowl

A child's drawing of her offerings to the Buddha.

11

What can you see?

There are many different kinds of **Buddhist** art. Most Buddhist pictures and objects are **symbols**. A symbol is a way of showing something without using words. This means that the **images** are not just for decoration, but to remind Buddhists of their beliefs.

The symbol most often used for **Buddhism** is a wheel with eight spokes. This reminds Buddhists of eight good ways they should try to live.

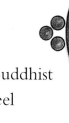

A Buddhist wheel

The lotus flower

The lotus flower is also used as a symbol for Buddhism. It grows in mud and dirty water but becomes a beautiful flower. It reminds Buddhists of how they can become pure. The **Buddha** is often shown sitting on a lotus flower.

Wheel of Life

The wheel is also used in this Tibetan Wheel of Life painting. Here the wheel shows how Buddhists are born again and again in six different worlds until they become **enlightened**. This illustrates the Buddhist belief in **reincarnation**.

Prayer wheels

In some temples you may see prayer wheels. Buddhists believe that as the prayer wheels turn, the many prayers written inside are repeated again and again to become more powerful.

The Wheel of Life

A prayer wheel

13

What do people do there?

Early morning is a good time of day for prayers. But many **Buddhists** meet in the evening after work and school, or on Sunday. A **Dharma** Centre usually arranges prayer meetings.

Puja

A prayer meeting is known as **puja**. People say prayers to the **Buddha** and often chant **mantras**. Mantras are special sayings. They help Buddhists to think deeply. Musicians may play simple music during parts of the puja. During some pujas food and drink are offered to everyone.

A puja in a temple.

Meditation

Buddhists believe that **meditation** can help anyone solve problems and find peace. Meditation means controlling your thoughts to quieten the mind. Buddhist temples are calm, peaceful places to help people meditate.

Try to meditate yourself. Sit comfortably and close your eyes. Concentrate on your breath as it goes in and out of your nose. When thoughts enter your mind try to 'let go' of them. Think about your breathing again. Try to do this for a few minutes. You will find it is not easy to control your thoughts, but with practice it gets easier!

A Buddhist girl meditates in front of a **shrine**.

Teachings in the temple

Buddhists also come to the temple to learn from the **scriptures**. These are the words of the **Buddha**. They were written down by his followers after he died. They wrote down his teachings so that they would not be lost.

Scriptures are usually written on sheets of paper and wrapped in cloth. The Buddha gave 84,000 teachings about the path to **enlightenment**.

These are typical temple scriptures.

Temple teachers

Buddhists believe that if you study the scriptures carefully and **meditate** often, you will become very wise. Buddhists usually learn about the scriptures in a temple or **shrine** room. The teachers often sit higher than the students on what is sometimes called a throne.

There are many Buddhist teachers. Tibetans call their teachers **lamas**. Some Buddhists believe their teachers are enlightened, just like the Buddha.

This is the Dalai Lama, the religious leader of the Tibetan people.

Special events

One of the most important ceremonies that takes place in a temple or **shrine** room is the refuge ceremony. A refuge is a safe place. **Buddhists** believe that their safest refuge is the **Three Jewels**. When someone decides to become a Buddhist, they call it 'taking refuge'.

Buddhist teachers lead the refuge ceremony. The person wishing to become a Buddhist says prayers to the Three Jewels and makes promises to try to become **enlightened**.

A refuge ceremony.

Buddha Day

Buddha Day is the day when Buddha's followers remember his life. It is also known as Wesak. The temple is decorated in a special way on this day. People bring beautiful flowers and burn special **incense**.

People also light candles. The candlelight reminds them that the Buddha's teachings help them to see important things about life. A teacher may tell the story of the life of the Buddha. Buddhists try to be especially good on Buddha Day.

Buddhist children bring flowers to the temple for the Wesak festival.

Other peaceful places

As well as temples, there are other places and buildings where **Buddhists** go to **meditate** and pray. Most Buddhists have a place in their home which is a **shrine** to the **Buddha**.

There are also gardens which are specially designed to help people think deeply about life, and to feel peaceful and calm. Some Buddhists go on a **retreat**. They go to special, peaceful places where they can spend a lot of time meditating.

Peace **pagodas**, like this one in London, are built by Japanese Buddhists as **symbols** of peace amongst all religions.

Stupas

Stupas are a type of building which is shaped like a rounded hill. They are designed to make Buddhists think of **enlightenment**. There are many of them in Asia and a few in Britain.

Monasteries and nunneries

Ordained Buddhists are called **monks** and **nuns**. They often live in a **monastery** or **nunnery**. Monks and nuns make extra vows to try to lead a very religious life. They study and meditate a lot. Many Buddhists visit monasteries and nunneries to learn more about **Buddhism** and meditation.

A Buddhist monk teaching children.

Glossary

The letters in brackets help you to say some words.

Buddha (buh–dah) founder of Buddhism who lived 2500 years ago and gave us the teachings on how to become enlightened

buddhas other beings who some Buddhists believe have become enlightened

Buddhism religion begun by the Buddha in India

Buddhist person who follows the religion of Buddhism

Dharma (DAR–mah) teachings of the Buddha. Also known as 'the Truth' or the way to enlightenment.

enlightened/enlightenment state of perfect happiness and understanding, beyond all suffering and pain.

incense sticks of perfumed substances such as herbs and spices which can be burned slowly to make a place smell pleasant

image picture or holy statue of the Buddha or one of the buddhas

lama (LAR–mah) means teacher. It is a respectful title given to Tibetan teachers who are believed to be holy and wise

mantra special words which are meant to be powerful, especially if repeated

meditate/meditation sitting in silence and trying to clear and control the mind and only think about special things

monastery place where monks (ordained Buddhist men) live

monk man who makes special Buddhist promises to live an especially good life

nun woman who makes special Buddhist promises to live an especially good life

nunnery place where nuns (ordained Buddhist women) live

offering object placed on a shrine to encourage kindness, generosity and respect

ordained taking special promises called vows to live a very religious life

pagoda (pag–oh–dah) building designed to feel like a place of refuge and peace

prostrate bowing to a holy image or person by lying on the ground

puja (POO–jah) word for prayer in the old Indian language of Sanskrit

reincarnation Buddhist belief that we are reborn again and again until we reach enlightenment

retreat stopping your routine for a while to mainly meditate and pray

Sangha (SAN–gah) Buddhist teachers, monks and nuns

scriptures written words of the Buddha, remembered by his followers and written down after his death. These have been copied and translated into many languages.

shrine special place where Buddhists place holy objects

symbol picture or object which tells us something without using words

Three Jewels the three most respected things in Buddhism: the Buddha, the Dharma and the Sangha

Two main Buddhist groups

The two main groups of Buddhists follow slightly different teachings.

Theravada Buddhists follow the original teachings of the Buddha. They use the older spellings of Buddhist words. For instance, instead of Dharma they say Dhamma.

Mahayana Buddhists say that the original teachings of the Buddha are not the only teachings. They believe that there are more teachings from other enlightened beings which are also important. They use the more modern spellings of Buddhist words. This book uses these spellings because there are more of these kinds of Buddhists in Britain today.

Index